Photographs
Colin Jeal
David Gree[n]
Dick Mills
David Alderton

Front cover painting by:
Julie Stooks

Your First
TERRAPIN

CONTENTS

Red Eared Terrapins 4
Equipment........................8
Filtrations 9
Heating 12
Basking Sites 13
Lighting........................15
Decor and Substrates 17

Safety 19
Food and Feeding...............21
Health 23
Breeding 25
Buying..........................26
Species Selection...............27
Bibliography 33

©1996
by Kingdom
Books
PO7 6AR
ENGLAND

your first terrapin

Kingdom Books is an imprint of T.F.H. Publications   Printed in England.

RED EARED TERRAPINS

your first terrapin **RED EARED TERRAPINS**

Baby red eared terrapins are very sweet and appealing, especially to children who see them as 'ninja turtles' and as playthings. However, whilst terrapins are cute as babies they can grow into 25cm animals that require a large tank and specialist heating, lighting and filtration, all of which can be very expensive. You also have to provide quite a lot of space for them. If terrapins are not looked after properly they become smelly, and need cleaning out every few days just to make them bearable to live with.

Terrapins make very responsive and interesting pets, that give a wonderful insight into the aquatic environment. By aquascaping and using plants above the water level, you can create a beautiful living picture in your living room rivalling an aquarium of tropical fish.

A hatchling painted terrapin. There are several subspecies of this terrapin, and they are all very similar.

RED EARED TERRAPINS   your first terrapin

As long as you are prepared to spend the time and money it takes to look after terrapins properly, they will be easy-to-keep, long-lived pets. Many owners even become emotionally attached to their terrapins.

In the past, millions of red eared terrapins have been sold by uncaring or just plain ignorant dealers, who provide nothing but a cheap plastic turtle bowl, dried tubifex worms and a plastic palm tree. This kind of set up is, of course, totally unsuitable for baby terrapins and most of those treated in this way are sure to die within a few months. No animals should be treated like this and it is up to pet owners to have a responsible attitude towards any animal they are in charge of.

Also, parents should ensure that any animal bought for their children is looked after properly. Too many terrapins have been bought for children who lose interest as the terrapins grow and are no longer cute. Cleaning soon becomes a chore, and left to the parents. It does not take long for the parents to lose interest also, and try to get rid of the unfortunate creature.

Finding homes for large terrapins is not easy. Most zoos, pet shops and rescue centres are full up, and cannot take in any more. Unfortunately, when a home cannot be found, too many people release the unwanted animal into the wild. Many ponds around the country seem to have a terrapin in residence and, if the numbers carry on increasing, serious harm may be caused to our natural plant and animal species.

The area in America that the terrapins cover reaches as far north as Canada and as far south as Mexico, so terrapins can adapt easily to most habitats. They can hibernate if it gets too cold over the winter and emerge in the spring. If ever they were to breed in this country, they could cause severe ecological problems. Under the Wildlife and Countryside Act 1981, it is illegal to release any non-native animal into the wild.

Here is a basic list of issues to think about before purchasing a terrapin. Once purchased, terrapins should be with you for the rest of their lives, as should any animal. You must be willing to spend money on providing a home for your terrapins, with light, heat and filtration. You must be prepared to feed them a wide variety of good quality food. You must clean out the tanks and service the filters regularly.

If you think you can cope with all these responsibilities, then you will be rewarded with a beautiful addition to your home in the form of a hardy, interesting and long-lived pet.

In America, all terrapins and turtles, including the marine species, are called turtles, and the red ears and their close relations are referred to as sliders. In the UK, most of the species that live on both land and in fresh water are called terrapins and those that live in the sea, turtles.

As it is almost certain that you will start by keeping red eared terrapins, this book describes the keeping of this species. Red eared terrapins are **Chelonians**, which is the order of animals that includes the tortoises, terrapins and marine turtles. The family is **Emydidae** and their Latin name is *Trachemys scripta elegans*. About fourteen sub-species are believed to exist at the present time. Many of the terrapins imported into the UK are captive-bred in the Far East. Adults reach a size of approximately 12.5-17.5cm in shell length, although the record is 25cm. Females grow larger than the males.

When mature, a male terrapin develops long claws on its front feet and it also has a much longer and thicker tail than in the female. If looked after properly, terrapins can live for up to 30 years. In recent years many colour varieties have been developed, including albino (lacking all pigment), ornates (with bright yellow markings on the shell), and pastel (red markings and patterns on the upper shell). Some red eared terrapins become much darker as they get older and some lose the characteristic red markings on the side of the head.

Most red eared terrapins are captive bred or captive farmed. In the USA and Far East, terrapin farms have been created, that is, natural ponds are fenced off for the sole purpose of raising baby terrapins.

RED EARED TERRAPIN   **your first terrapin**

Red eared terrapins have been known to grow as large as 25cm (10in), so bear this in mind when you are thinking about their housing.

    Unfortunately, most of the more unusual or rare terrapins are still taken from the wild. A captive-bred baby or juvenile terrapin is likely to do much better in captivity than a wild-caught specimen which is usually highly stressed and full of parasites.

    Before buying your terrapin, you need to set up its home. This needs to be done at least three days before you bring home your new pet, to ensure that the filtration and heating are working and that the water is warm enough.

EQUIPMENT

your first terrapin **EQUIPMENT**

The main requirement for terrapins are: a tank or enclosure as big as possible, clean water, a completely dry area where they can bask out of the water, a heat source, lighting, correct feeding, regular maintenance, care of filter and waste removal.

The first piece of equipment to acquire is the tank or enclosure that you intend to use for your terrapins. The most popular terrapin home is the glass aquarium. It is very practical and looks good in the home, is fairly cheap to purchase and available at any aquatic shop. The minimum size for hatchlings is 60 x 30 x 30cm.

Although a tank 60cm long is a minimum, bear in mind that terrapins soon grow and will need a much larger tank. A pair of adult terrapins need a tank which is at least 120cm long, 45cm wide and deep enough to provide a water depth of 20-25cm. Always purchase the largest tank your home and pocket will allow, so you do not have to replace the tank and equipment as the terrapins grow. With the variety of styles and sizes available, you are sure to find something to suit your home and, with a bit of imagination, create a centrepiece for your room.

The other way to house your terrapin is to use a small pond. You can use pre-formed fibreglass which comes in a variety of shapes and sizes, either building it into the corner of a room or into the garden for summer use. A terrapin kept in the garden must be in a secure enclosure to prevent it escaping, and there must be some land around the pond for basking. Never use a small plastic bowl for terrapins as this is not the correct environment.

The single most often-quoted reason people give for wanting to get rid of their terrapins is that the animals always smell horrible, are constantly dirty and need cleaning out. This may be true of neglected terrapins in unfiltered tanks but, if looked after properly, they should never smell.

Terrapins are voracious feeders, and the food is often ripped apart and makes quite a mess. To keep the main tank clean, you can remove the terrapins from their home tank to a separate feeding tank. You must ensure that the water is the same temperature, but it can be thrown away after feeding along with the mess. Normally, the main tank will need cleaning once a week. Use a syphon tube to syphon out just the waste or completely empty the tank and replace all the water. Syphons are very simple pieces of equipment, but try to purchase one with an automatic starting system. Dirty terrapin water is not very pleasant and could be harmful.

FILTRATION

FILTRATION your first terrapin

There are five different types of filters available for use with terrapins:

1. Internal power filters   2. External power filters   3. Undergravel filters
4. Air operated sponge filters   5. Pond filters

INTERNAL POWER FILTER

The internal power filter consists of a small, submersible water pump which draws the water through a cartridge of foam or sponge. This is the best form of filtration for terrapins, as it is easily accessible and simple to clean. Whenever you do a water change, remove the filter and rinse it out in the old water to preserve the bacteria. The main drawback of this filter is that it takes up space inside the tank and, although most come with suckers to hold them in place, large terrapins dislodge them easily, leaving the filter to float around the tank and look unsightly. It is simple to lay these filters down and so reduce the depth of water they need. I have used these filters on their side for many years without any problems. The advantage is that they are relatively inexpensive compared with other filters.

EXTERNAL POWER FILTER

The external power filter works on the same principle as the internal power filter, using a water pump to draw water through the filtration media. The main difference is that it is housed outside the tank, and the filter media is cased inside a watertight plastic canister. The water is taken from the tank through plastic tubes. External filters are a little more versatile than internal filters, as the extra space for the filtration media allows other forms to be used such as foam, ceramic media, and filter wool. The main advantage of using this type of filter, however, is that all that goes inside the tank is the two plastic tubes that take the water in and out of the tank. One make of external filter includes a heater inside the filter, eliminating the need for a heater in the tank.

These filters are much more expensive than the internal power filter, and they can be tricky to clean out. The feed tubes pass under the tank and so are under water pressure. Consequently, they need some sort of tap system to enable the filter to be opened without water going all over the floor. It can be difficult to get the sealing rings in place to prevent leaks. I always stand canister filters in a small washing-up bowl to prevent water leaking on the carpet. As these filters contain a lot more media they can be left for slightly longer between servicing than the internal filters.

UNDERGRAVEL FILTER

Although an undergravel filter may look good initially, it is not really much use in maintaining terrapins, as it soon becomes blocked by faeces and requires huge amounts of maintenance. If the filter is not maintained 'dead spots' form, which can go black and smelly. An undergravel filter consists of a plate that sits on the bottom of the tank under the gravel layer. The water is drawn through the gravel either by the use of a submersible water pump or an air uplift. Generally, I would not recommend the use of undergravel filters with terrapins.

SPONGE FILTER

In principle, this is similar to the internal canister filter, except that the water is drawn directly through the sponge using air from an aquarium air pump. The water needs to be fairly deep for the air uplift to work. The only problem that I have encountered with this filter is that some terrapins, especially larger ones, bite chunks out of the sponge, which is dangerous and can kill them if they eat it. It is better to use one of the canister filters described above.

FILTRATION

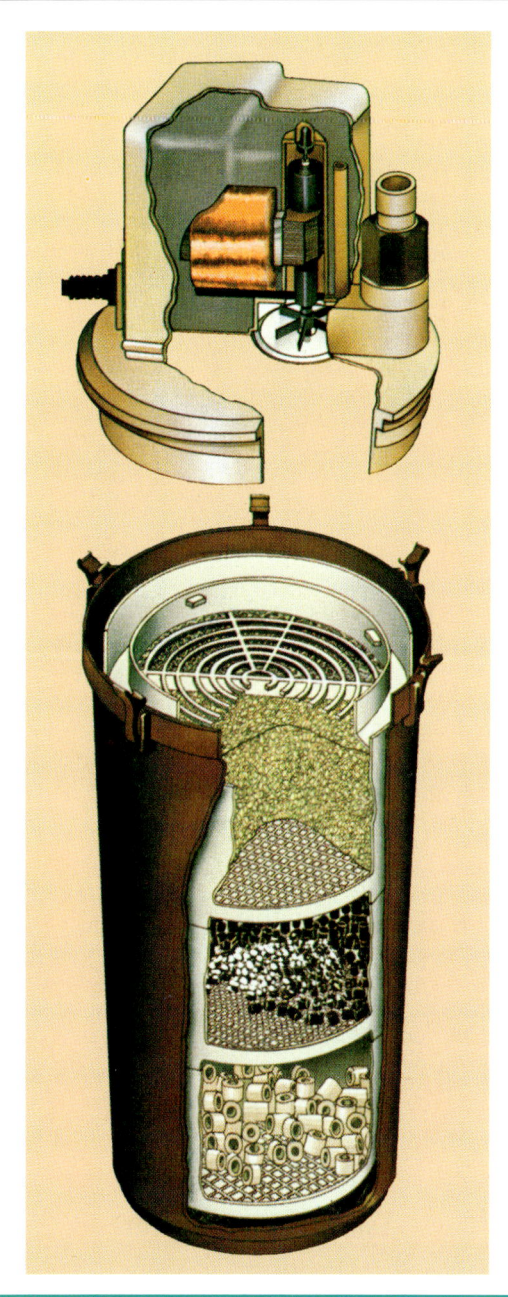

POND FILTER

A pond filter is usually a domestic water tank filled with media such as layers of open-celled foam, hortag, plastic media, or one of the new ceramic type media. This type of filter is available in all sizes up to 6000 gallons, although you are not likely to have a pond of this size. These filters require a submersible pond pump to operate them and can be quite expensive to buy. Pond filters can also be purchased with ultra violet light systems which kill the water-borne algae that turn the water green. They may also have some effect in cutting down some water-borne diseases organisms.

Left: A cut-away view of a typical external power filter. The types of filter media may be changed depending upon need and usage.

Far left: A red eared terrapin.

HEATING

Baby terrapins should be kept in water where the temperature is between 25 and 29°C. As adults the terrapins can be kept at temperatures between 23 and 26°C.

There are two main methods of heating a terrapin tank. The first is to use an aquarium heater thermostat, which has the heating element and the thermostat housed together in a glass tube, and is submersed in the water. Some manufacturers use a combination of plastic and metal in the production of their heaters, which are much safer to use in the terrapin tank as there is less risk of them being broken by the terrapins.

Submersible heaters must be protected from the terrapins for two reasons. The first is to stop the terrapins breaking the heater, and the second is to prevent them burning themselves on it. I have seen some very nasty thermal burns on the plastron (bottom of the shell) of red eared terrapins. There is a heater guard on the market that can be used with small terrapins, but you will probably need to construct a more substantial guard for use with larger terrapins.

Heater guards can be made from plastic-coated wire or an air brick, the type used in wall ventilation and available from builders' merchants. Probably the best method of heating a terrapin tank is to use an undertank heat mat. This must be of a type suitable for use with aquaria and not for reptiles. The heat mat must be connected to an external electronic thermostat with a waterproof temperature probe, available from aquatic shops. When choosing the heater, be sure to select the correct wattage for the size of tank, ie, 75-100 watt for a 60cm tank rising to a 200 watt for a 120cm tank and over.

Do not keep your terrapins at temperatures between 18°C and 22°C as they will neither hibernate nor feed properly. This will result in either pneumonia or the animal starving to death. It is important to use a thermometer to measure the water temperature. Digital electronic thermometers are the best type to use, as they have a probe which goes in the water, with the rest of it sticking to the outside of the tank for easy reading. Liquid crystal thermometers that stick on the outside of the tank are cheap, but not as accurate as the other types of thermometer.

BASKING SITES

BASKING SITES your first terrapin

Your terrapins need to have access to dry land where they can climb out of the water and bask. Make a dry site without taking away any water area by suspending a sheet of wood over one end of the tank above the water, with a wooden ramp for the terrapins to climb up.

More elaborate structures can be made using rocks, gravel or slate to form the land area but, if possible, try not to use up too much water

A large, female red eared terrapin enjoying the outdoor sun.

BASKING SITES

space. The land area must be big enough for the terrapins to move around comfortably. Always make sure the ramp is not at too much of an angle, as terrapins are not the best of climbers.

Make sure that rocks cannot be dislodged by the terrapins. If a terrapin was trapped under water by a falling rock, eventually it would drown. Falling rocks can also crack your tank, causing total mayhem!

One of the best methods for making a land area is to use house bricks or ornamental walling bricks found in garden centres (these usually have rounded edges), placed in two piles until the desired height is reached. A heavy piece of slate can be placed across the top, with more slate for the ramp.

Cork bark can be used as an interim measure, as it soon becomes waterlogged and sinks. Bogwood and mopani tree root available from aquatic shops can also be used, and are very ornamental.

A cheap plastic pond makes an escape-proof summer enclosure.

LIGHTING

LIGHTING   your first terrapin

Terrapins greatly appreciate a light above the basking site. They love to bask under a heat source, spreading their feet out as if sunbathing. If you have more than one terrapin, they will pile on top of each other in order to get closer to the heat source. Do not let them get too close or touch the light bulb, or they may get burnt.

    The best form of light is an incandescent spot light. Place the bulb above a sliding glass cover (not a plastic condensation cover as this will melt), as accidents can happen easily. Once I walked past one of my terrapin tanks and frightened a basking African mud turtle which launched itself into the water for cover. This created quite a splash, and water droplets hit the light bulb, causing it to explode and shower glass over the terrapin tank. Cover the bulb and be safe rather than sorry.

Two terrapins on an astroturf-covered basking platform. The indented markings on the shell of the turtle in the foreground could be a sign of a disease such as shell rot.

your first terrapin — **LIGHTING**

Artificial lighting using a full spectrum bulb such as the new reptiglow bulb is probably beneficial, but does not seem to be essential for the raising of terrapins. Although some species may require ultra violet (UV) light, very little work has been done to assess exactly which species these are. It can be used to create 'day and night', and enables you to view your terrapins' behaviour fully.

Some reptiles need UV lighting so that they can synthesize vitamin D3, essential for health, but this does not seem to be the case with terrapins. I have raised many terrapins to adulthood successfully with only a good diet and proper care.

The Stinkpot, *Sternotherus odoratus*, gets its name from the foul smell it produces to ward off aggressors.

DECOR AND SUBSTRATES

DECOR AND SUBSTRATES your first terrapin

The easiest way to maintain a tank is to keep the bottom bare. It is very easy to clean as the water and all the muck can be syphoned out from the bottom without having to worry about sucking up gravel or stones.

Most keepers, however, use large grade gravel or, better still, small round pebbles. Fine gravel or sand can be used but are far from ideal, as waste can be harboured, building up large numbers of harmful bacteria, and the sand can also get into and harm the pumps on canister filters.

Rocks or bogwood in the tank must be firmly anchored so the terrapins cannot dislodge them, as already discussed. Anything that you place in the tank must be smooth, as any rough edges may cause damage to your pets.

Being omnivorous, most terrapins eat any plants placed within their reach. You can use plastic plants, but only use tough plastic plants as terrapins will try to eat them.

Above the water and out of reach of the terrapins you can use plants like Bromeliads, air plants and various tree climbing plants such as cheese plants and most moisture-loving house plants. Only your imagination can limit the effect you want. You could try to make a waterfall, or even re-create a tropical rainforest in miniature.

Note the long claws of this male terrapin. The knobbly appearance of the shell was caused by poor nutrition when the animal was younger.

your first terrapin — **DECOR AND SUBSTRATES**

Try to choose smooth rocks for basking sites.

SAFETY

SAFETY | **your first terrapin**

Safety precautions should always be taken when you work around the tank, because of the various electrical appliances.

Always turn off all the electrical appliances before putting your hands in the water. If you are going to expose the element on the heater, turn it off 15 minutes before you take it out of the water, allowing it to cool down so it does not shatter.

Red eared terrapins have been blamed for infecting people with salmonella, mainly in the USA. I have been keeping terrapins for over 20 years, and have never suffered from salmonella, or know of anyone in the United Kingdom who can prove they caught salmonella from their terrapins. However, even though the risk of salmonella is extremely rare it is there, so practise strict hygiene and wash your hands whenever you come into contact with terrapins. Because of the salmonella scare, in the 1970s the USA banned the sale of terrapins under a shell length of 10cm and that ban is still in force.

Children must be supervised around terrapins, not only to make sure they wash their hands, but to make sure the terrapins do not confuse little fingers with worms and bite them.

An adult painted terrapin showing beautiful markings.

your first terrapin **SAFETY**

Close-up of a painted terrapin showing the beautiful stripes. Note the hard, bill-like mouth.

FOOD AND FEEDING

FOOD AND FEEDING *your first terrapin*

Most terrapins are omnivorous, which means they eat virtually anything. Your main consideration is to provide a good variety of foods.

There are numerous commercial foods available, usually pelleted or as sticks. These should be used only as part of the diet and never as the sole food for any terrapin. Canned terrapin foods are now appearing in the shops, but these can be messy to use.

Frozen fish can be fed; the best types are found in packs in aquatic shops and include whitebait and lancefish. Feed these whole as the bones and guts are a good source of calcium, vitamins and minerals. You can also obtain live tubifex and bloodworms from your local aquatic shop, which are particularly good for hatchlings. You can also use freeze dried foods, such as brineshrimp, tubifex, bloodworm and krill.

One of the best and cheapest foods is earthworms dug from your garden. Earthworms are high in protein and terrapins adore them. Do make sure that no pesticides or chemicals have been used in the area where you collect your worms. Mealworms available from reptile shops can be given as a treat, but not too often.

Meat can be used in moderation, but avoid fatty meats. Heart is the best, but only ever give it in small amounts. You can use chicken offal, but always cook it thoroughly first to avoid any risk of salmonella.

Dog and cat foods can be used but avoid tinned stuffs which can be very messy. Dry dog or cat foods should be soaked before feeding.

Fresh or frozen prawns and cockles can be fed and prawn shells are especially helpful for colour enhancement and calcium content.

Most terrapins will take plant matter in the form of lettuce, banana, watercress and duckweed. Some prefer more plant matter in their diet as they get older. There are now frozen foods on the market which combine all the above. They are good but may prove expensive, especially as the terrapins get bigger.

VITAMINS AND MINERALS

Terrapins need vitamins and minerals to keep healthy, and this is best achieved by using one of the specialist reptile vitamin powders now available. Put the powder inside a food such as lancefish, to ensure the terrapin gets it before it dissolves in the water. Follow the manufacturer's recommended quantities on the packet, and do not exceed them.

your first terrapin   **FOOD AND FEEDING**

The calcium that terrapins need for their shells (and for egg production in the case of breeding females), can be provided by cuttlefish bones. Cuttlefish is available from any pet shop and can be floated in the water. The terrapins will bite chunks off. You can also buy calcium blocks specifically made for terrapins, although these are quite small, which again are placed in the water.

Pelleted colour-enhancing foods as used for fish can be fed if your terrapins' colour seems to be fading. These foods contain carotene which will help restore and keep your terrapins' colour, although it is not essential for good health.

The False Map terrapin, *Graptemys pseudogeographica*, can be a fussy eater but, once it has started eating, causes its keeper very little trouble.

HEALTH

There is not room in this book for a detailed discussion on terrapin diseases, but the following will help you diagnose some common ailments.

SOFT SHELL

Soft shell is also known as metabolic bone disease and is caused by a lack of calcium or an unbalanced calcium/phosphorous ratio and/or vitamin D3 deficiency. The symptom is softening of the shell, usually starting in the rear marginal scutes (back upper edges of the shell). Prolonged exposure to this problem leads to paralysed rear legs, deformities of the shell and, eventually, death. You should never encounter this disease if you follow the proper feeding regime described in this book. This problem can be treated easily by restoring a correct diet with vitamin and calcium supplements. If the terrapin is in a very bad state, a vet can inject calcium and vitamins.

RESPIRATORY INFECTIONS

Respiratory infections are characterised by snuffly breathing, closed or swollen eyes, loss of appetite and bubbly mucus from the nostrils or mouth. An affected terrapin sits at the basking site with its neck outstretched and its mouth open, making choking noises. Often one of the first signs is that the terrapin swims lop-sided because the lung on that side is full of mucus. This pneumonia-like infection can usually be cured by raising the temperature to around 29-36°C for about a week. If the animal's condition deteriorates, or it is not better by the end of one week, consult your vet.

SHELL AND SKIN INFECTIONS (SHELL ROT)

Shell rot is caused by bacteria or a fungus. It shows up as soft, discoloured patches on the shell, usually containing a cheesy substance. Treat this by cleaning out the 'cheese' and painting the lesion with a proprietary iodine-type reptile wound treatment. Skin damage can be treated in the same way. Use a proprietary bacterial and fungus treatment suitable for tropical fish, at double strength. Again, if you are unsure, consult a vet.

SWOLLEN EYES

This disease is caused by a lack of vitamin A as a result of poor diet. The symptoms are swelling and closure of the eyelids caused by inflammation of the tear ducts. Long-term treatment is to improve the diet and give a vitamin supplement. More immediate treatment is a vitamin injection given by a vet. Swelling of the eyes is also a sign of other diseases and problems, so make sure your terrapin is not displaying any other symptoms.

PARASITES

Terrapins do not seem to suffer with external parasites, but wild-caught animals especially can suffer from internal ones. Symptoms include listlessness, non-feeding, loss of weight, and runny, bloody or mucus-like faeces. As these symptoms can also be true of bacterial or protozoan infections, it is very important to get the affected animal to a specialist reptile vet for treatment.

EAR INFECTIONS

Ear infections are fairly rare, but occasionally you see the characteristic swelling on one or both sides of the head. Again, this needs to be treated by a specialist reptile vet as soon as possible.

A female red ear (right) and a male yellow belly (left).

BREEDING

BREEDING *your first terrapin*

Kept under proper conditions, most red ears will try to breed. The male does a fascinating and quite comical courtship display, tickling the female's cheeks with his long claws until she gives in to being mated.

Approximately one to two weeks after a successful mating, the female will lay a clutch of eggs. This can number up to 25 eggs, although ten or under is more usual.

Provide an egg laying site in the form of a large container of damp sand, or the female will lay her eggs in the water. This alone will kill the eggs, but the terrapins will eat them, leaving you to pick out small pieces of shell from the bottom of the tank.

Any eggs that the female lays should be incubated at a temperature of 26-27°C, and should hatch in 55 to 65 days. To try and bring terrapins into breeding condition it is worth hibernating them. They need a temperature of 10-15°C for a period of 6-8 weeks starting in January. This allows proper egg and sperm development.

A successful mating will result in eggs like this one.

BUYING

your first terrapin BUYING

The first thing to do when looking for a terrapin is to travel around your local aquarium and reptile shops. You are looking for well-kept animals that have clean water and lots of space, and which look alert and healthy.

Knowledgeable, helpful staff are also essential. Ask some questions about the basic husbandry of terrapins. Test the staff to see if they know about the care of terrapins or are likely to sell you anything, such as a plastic turtle bowl, just to get your money. A shop that puts you off terrapins rather than make a sale has a genuine concern for the animals and is far more likely to give you the correct advice. The shop staff should make it clear to any prospective purchaser the possible size and housing requirements of the species they are interested in.

When you have selected a shop you are happy with (and be prepared to travel some distance to find one), and have your tank set up and waiting, you can now proceed to purchase your terrapin or terrapins.

A healthy terrapin will be basking or looking for food. Ask to handle the terrapin; it should feel heavy for its size. Gently pull on the hind foot and the animal should respond immediately by strongly pulling its foot back in.

The mouth and nostrils should be clean with no liquid of any kind coming from them. The eyes must be clear and bright; reject any terrapin with swollen or closed eyes. Look for strange lumps on the head or other parts of the body, as these may be the start of major problems.

The shell should be whole with no wounds or chunks missing. Avoid terrapins with light or dark patches on the shell as these may be bacterial or fungus infections.

The shell should be hard and not flexible. A soft shell is a sign of metabolic bone disease and any animal with a flexible shell should be left in the shop, unless it is a hatchling. Sometimes a very young terrapin is imported with its egg tooth still on the nose. If you find one this young usually the shell will still be slightly soft. This is natural and the shell should harden up within a few weeks. Look at the other terrapins and you will find that some of the shells are already hard.

SPECIES SELECTION

SPECIES SELECTION   your first terrapin

Most of the following species, with a few exceptions, can be kept in the same way as red ears. Some species can be kept together, while others are not suitable for mixing with others. As a general rule, keep terrapins of the same size and vigour together, such as red ears, cooters, yellow and red bellies. Maps and painted terrapins can be kept together as can mud and musk terrapins. When keeping different species together, keep an eye on the animals to ensure they are all healthy, not being bullied and are all getting enough food. Do not be tempted to try and keep baby and adult terrapins together. When feeding time comes, babies can get eaten or severely bitten during the feeding frenzy.

RED EARED TERRAPIN (*TRACHEMY SCRIPTA ELEGANS*)

This is the most common and cheapest terrapin available. Conditions for its keeping are described throughout this book. It is the least troublesome and most hardy, and is always captive bred or farmed.

RED AND YELLOW BELLIED TERRAPIN (*PSEUDEMYS NELLSONI AND CONCINNA*)

These are closely related to the red ears and need similar care. There are lots of colour varieties depending on where they are caught.

PAINTED TERRAPIN (*CHRYSEMYS PICTA*)

Painted terrapins are similar to red ears. The females can grow up to 25cm long. Sexing and diet are similar to the red ears and these are the next best starter terrapin. There are several different sub-species but they all look similar, being suffused with red and yellow markings and lacking the characteristic red ear.

MAP AND FALSE MAP TERRAPIN (*GRAPTEMYS*)

This beautiful, if rather strange-looking terrapin, with its brownish shell and small head, can be kept in the same way as red ears, but not with them. Maps are a little more delicate than other terrapins. The males are smaller than the females, which grow to around 15-17.5cm.

SOFT SHELLED TURTLES (*TRIONYX*)

There are two main types of soft shelled turtles imported into the UK. You see more of the common, Far Eastern species *Trionyx sinensis*. These are

your first terrapin   SPECIES SELECTION

'Picta' means 'painted', and this is the species name given to the Painted Terrapin.

very cute, bright orange-bellied babies, but become big and aggressive. They try to eat anything, so cannot be kept with any other species and you must be very careful with your fingers! The American species is very similar to the oriental turtle, but can grow even bigger, some reaching 60-90cm in diameter.

These animals seldom come out of the water and need a substrate of soft sand which, if not kept scrupulously clean, will cause shell rot problems.

MUD AND MUSK TERRAPINS *(KINOSTERNON)*

These gorgeous little terrapins are often underrated. Most of the species do not grow more than 10cm. This means they can be kept in smaller aquariums, which is a great advantage if you are limited for space. The other advantage is that they do not eat plants, so a very attractive set-up can be achieved. Their care is the same as for red ears, but do not mix them with other species.

SPECIES SELECTION   *your first terrapin*

Above: The Mississippi Mud Turtle can be identified by the two yellow lines on its head.
Below: This is *Chelydra serpentina*, the smaller of the species of Snapping Turtle

your first terrapin   **SPECIES SELECTION**

Above: The American variety of Softshell Turtle can grow up to 90cm in diameter.
Below: The European Pond Tortoise is a hardy animal, but does not often breed in captivity.

SPECIES SELECTION
your first terrapin

STINKPOT TURTLES (KINOSTERNON ODORATUM)

Stinkpot turtles are like musk terrapins, but have a yellow stripe down the neck. The babies usually are available when they are about the size of a coffee bean. However, they are quite difficult to raise from this size.

SNAPPING TURTLES (CHELYDRA)

Snapping turtles look like prehistoric monsters. They can grow to over 90kg in weight and are extremely nasty. Two species are available, the Common snapper *Chelydra serpentina*, which is the smaller of the two, and the Alligator snapper *Maroclemys temmincki*, the giant! Do not consider owning either of these turtles unless you are prepared to give lots of space and huge amounts of food to these very beautiful (depending on your point of view), but potentially very dangerous, nasty creatures.

This view of the underside of a Redbelly Terrapin (*Pseudemys rubriventris*) shows how it got its name.

AFRICAN SIDENECK AND MUD TURTLES (PELOMEDUSA AND PELUSIOS) SPECIES

These species are very similar to the musk and mud turtles from America. They grow to 15-25cm and are wonderful characters. Their housing and husbandry are the same as for the red ear.

EUROPEAN POND TORTOISE (EMYS OBICULARIS)

Over the past few years the European pond tortoise has been appearing for sale with more regularity. This beautiful, but expensive, animal should be kept in the same way as the red ear. In the south of England it can be kept outside all year round, as long as it has a deep pond. It is believed to have inhabited England before the Ice Age. This terrapin will grow to about 25cm long.

A red ear in typical pose, with its eyes and nostrils protruding from the surface of the water.

BIBLIOGRAPHY

ENCYCLOPEDIA OF TURTLES
Dr Peter C. H. Pritchard
ISBN 0-87666-918-6
TFH H-1011

Encyclopedia of Turtles is the first truly comprehensive standard reference work on all living turtles and terrapins, together with their subspecies.

Hardcover: 212 x 135mm, 895 pages, fully illustrated with colour and black and white photographs.

MAP TURTLES
W. P. Mara
ISBN 0-7938-2068-5
RE-156

Written by an experienced keeper, this handsome and colourful book provides all the information needed to keep both the map turtle and the Diamondback Terrapin.

Softcover: 250 x 170mm, 64 pages, fully illustrated with colour photographs.

COOTERS, SLIDERS AND PAINTED TURTLES
Jerry G. Walls
ISBN 0-7938-2069-3
RE-146

This book offers a complete introduction to the care, breeding and natural history of some of the most popular turtles and terrapins in the world.

Softcover: 250 x 170mm, 64 pages, fully illustrated with high-quality colour photographs

TURTLES AS A NEW PET
Al David
ISBN: 0-86622-621-4
TU-013

This book is designed specifically for those new to the keeping of terrapins and turtles, and covers everything they need to know about these fascinating reptiles.

Softback: 214 x 172 mm, 62 pages, fully illustrated with colour photographs

If you are serious about terrapin keeping, why not join your local reptile society or the British Chelonia Society.

British Chelonia Society
PO Box 2163
London NW10 5HW

British Herpetological Society
c/o Zoological Society of London
Regents Park
London NW1 4RY
Tel: 0181 452 9578